DATE DUE

SANDRA DAY O'CONNOR

Independent Thinker

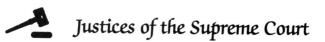 Justices of the Supreme Court

Sandra Day O'Connor

Independent Thinker

D. J. Herda

 Enslow Publishers, Inc.

40 Industrial Road   PO Box 38

Box 398   Aldershot

Berkeley Heights, NJ 07922   Hants GU12 6BP

USA   UK

http://www.enslow.com

Copyright © 1995 by D. J. Herda

Library of Congress Cataloging-in-Publication Data

Herda, D. J., 1948-
    Sandra Day O'Connor: independent thinker / D. J. Herda.
        p.   cm.— (Justices of the Supreme Court)
    Includes bibliographical references and index.
    Summary: A biography of the first woman Supreme Court Justice in
the United States.
        ISBN 0-89490-558-9
        1. O'Connor, Sandra Day, 1930—Juvenile literature. 2. United States.
Supreme Court—Biography—Juvenile literature. 3. Women judges—
United States—Biography—Juvenile literature.
    [1. O'Connor, Sandra Day, 1930– . 2. Judges. 3. United States.
Supreme Court—Biography. 4. Women—Biography.]
    I. Title. II. Series.
KF8745.025H47   1995
347.73'2634—dc20
[B]
[347.30735]
[B]   94-49566
                                                                        CIP
                                                                        AC

Printed in the United States of America

10 9 8 7 6 5 4 3

Photo Credits: "Collection of the Supreme Court of the United States", pp. 11, 31, 47, 71, 87; Library of Congress, pp. 38, 56, 62, 74; Markow Photography, "Collection of the Supreme Court of the United States", p. 82; Renee Bouchard, Close Up Foundation, p. 17; Robert S. Oakes, "Collection of the Supreme Court of the United States", p. 23.

Cover Photo: Collection, United States Supreme Court Historical Society

CONTENTS

A Justice Is Born

On June 17, 1981, Judge Sandra Day O'Connor entered her chambers at the Arizona Court of Appeals. She slipped into her chair and unfolded the newspaper lying on her desk. On the front page of the *Arizona Republic* was an article saying that Supreme Court Justice Potter Stewart had just announced his retirement. The article went on to state that Arizona Senator Dennis DeConcini had suggested to President Ronald Reagan that he nominate O'Connor to fill the open position.

The news did not shock her. It is common practice upon learning of a Justice's retirement that a senator suggests someone from his or her own state to fill the vacancy. It is also common practice that the president overlook such suggestions. Most often, he will nominate someone of his own choice to the position.

Besides, never in the two-hundred-year history of the

Court had there been a woman Supreme Court Justice. O'Connor shrugged the story off.

What O'Connor did not realize at the time was that, as early as April 1981, Reagan—upon learning of Stewart's planned retirement—had begun asking his presidential aides to draw up a list of the nation's most qualified female lawyers and judges to take Stewart's place. At the very top of the list was Sandra Day O'Connor.

For nearly two months, a secret Justice Department investigation into the background and current activities of the Arizona judge unfolded. When the investigation was finally complete, the president ordered Attorney General William French Smith to break the news to O'Connor that she was a leading contender for the position.

On June 25, Smith called O'Connor and set up a personal interview in Phoenix. Smith's chief counselor and several staff members held long conversations with O'Connor. The interviewers returned to Washington with positive comments about the prospective nominee.

"She really made it easy," one official was quoted as saying.[1]

Several days later, O'Connor got a call from the White House. She flew to Washington, D.C., and on July 1 met privately with Reagan in the Oval Office. After a forty-five-minute talk, Reagan told his aides to look no further. He'd found the right woman for the job.

"Without a doubt," said Reagan, "the most awesome appointment a president can make is to the United States Supreme Court. That is not to say I would appoint a woman merely to do so."[2]

Reagan then introduced Sandra Day O'Connor to the press. He said she was a woman who possessed those unique qualities of temperament, fairness, intellectual capacity, and devotion to the public good that characterized the 101 Justices who had come before her.

The nomination was not without its controversy. Reagan's most conservative supporters opposed the nomination, claiming that O'Connor's record as an Arizona judge had been frighteningly liberal. She had taken a moderate view of abortion when she was in the Arizona state legislature, and that put off both conservatives and antiabortion activists.

Most of America's leading women's groups, however, felt differently. They viewed the nomination of the first woman ever to the United States Supreme Court as the best thing that could possibly happen to women—and, in fact, to America.

O'Connor's nomination, according to Eleanor Smeal of the National Organization for Women (NOW), was "a major victory for women's rights."[3] Senator Edward Kennedy, a liberal from Massachusetts, agreed.

This praise was just the beginning of the appointment process. Although the president is empowered by the Constitution to nominate federal judges, those nominations are subject to approval by the Senate. With such a controversial figure presented to them, the Senate Judiciary Committee was fully prepared to grill the Court's newest nominee.

Sessions before the committee are often frustrating and upsetting to nominees. Questions range from lighthearted and personal to the most complex issues of philosophy, morality, and professional beliefs. Often nominees become frustrated and contradict themselves. Sometimes they lose their tempers. Some have stated their feelings or positions improperly, leading to still further questions and the chance for even more personal embarrassment.

O'Connor's sessions went as smoothly as anyone might

have imagined. She calmly answered questions concerning her beliefs about the law. She told the committee members that, in her view, judges were there to interpret laws, not to make them, which is the legislature's duty.

When questioned about how she would vote on certain issues as a Supreme Court Justice, O'Connor firmly but politely refused to respond. She insisted that it would be improper for her to speculate on such matters before they came before her on the bench.

While her responses did not please everyone on the committee, they were enough to win her Senate confirmation to the Court a few days later. The vote was 99 to 0.

On September 25, 1981, when Sandra Day O'Connor arrived at the United States Supreme Court building, every seat in the spectators' gallery was taken. At precisely 2:04 P.M., the two doors leading to the chamber swung open, and the crowd began to buzz. From one door strode the President of the United States—Ronald Reagan. From the other came O'Connor, ready at last to take the oath in order to become the 102nd Justice in Supreme Court history—and the first woman ever.

Everyone in the courtroom rose as the eight black-robed Justices approached the mahogany bench at which some of the world's most famous legal questions have been argued. The attorney general of the United States moved that the clerk read the commission from the president appointing Justice O'Connor. Chief Justice Warren E. Burger granted the motion, and the clerk proceeded. O'Connor then placed her hand on a Bible and repeated the Constitutional oath, the same words that have been used at the swearing-in of Justices nearly since the beginning of the Court:

O'Connor, here with former President Ronald Reagan, was the first woman ever appointed to the Supreme Court.

I, Sandra Day O'Connor, do solemnly swear that I will support and defend the Constitution of the United States against all enemies, foreign and domestic; that I will bear true faith and allegiance to the same; that I take this obligation freely, without any mental reservation or purpose of evasion; and that I will well and faithfully discharge the duties of the office on which I am about to enter. So help me God.[4]

After completing the oath of office, O'Connor slipped into a black robe and, under the watchful eyes of family, friends, and hundreds of Washington officials, walked to the far right-hand side of the bench where tradition reserves a seat for the Court's newest Justice. History was made.

2

In the Beginning

Harry and Ada Mae Day had talked about having a child. Times were difficult back then, following the great Wall Street Crash of 1929. Stock prices had collapsed, financial institutions went bankrupt, people lost their life's savings, and tens of thousands of workers found themselves jobless each month.

While the Days were trying to decide whether or not to have a child, Ada Mae discovered that she was pregnant. Now there was no doubt about it. They were going to have a baby. It was a scary thought in light of the rough times in which they lived. But one way or another, they would be just fine.

Harry Day had grown up on a ranch in the wide-open spaces of southeastern Arizona. The ranch had been founded by Harry's father, Henry, and Henry's business partner, Lane Fisher. Henry had put up the money to buy cattle, and Fisher had gone to Mexico where he purchased 6,000 head. He drove the cattle back across the scrublands of Texas into Arizona, where they were set loose to graze on the lush grass bordering the Gila River. The land, which at the time was public domain, meaning anyone could use it, eventually became the Day's ranch—all 170,000 acres of it.

Naming the ranch was easy. The cattle that Fisher had brought back were branded with the letter B lying on its side. Henry called the ranch "The Lazy B."

Life was difficult during those early days on the ranch. Henry and his wife, Alice, were forced to endure many hardships. The worst came when a flash flood destroyed their home and washed the family piano down a canyon. Henry found it several days later—or what was left of it. The Days rebuilt their home on higher ground, where it exists to this day.

But flash floods weren't the only problem the Day family faced on the ranch. While most of the Apache, who had lived in the area for years, had long since moved to the San Carlos reservation, one man—a strong-willed leader named Geronimo—refused to give up his ancestral grounds. For years, Geronimo led Apache raids on white ranches and settlements in the area. Although the Days managed to escape personal injury, they lost forty-five horses to Apache war parties.

Finally, in 1886, after having been chased throughout the Southwest for more than a decade, Geronimo surrendered to the United States Army and was imprisoned. Twelve years later, in 1898, Sandra's father, Harry, was born.

Life on the ranch for young Harry was filled with hard work nearly twelve months a year. From riding the range and rounding up cattle to mending fences and putting up hay, there were always chores to be done.

There were fun times, too: sitting around the campfire and singing songs; reading by the light of a single candle;

learning to cook; and helping to deliver the young calves each spring. These were times that Harry enjoyed most. They were so permanently etched in his memory that—except for a short period in which he lived in Pasadena, California—he made the ranch his home for life.

As Harry grew into manhood, he began looking for a wife. He had known a neighbor girl—Ada Mae Wilke—on and off for years. She had traveled to Europe when she was sixteen and, two years later, left the Wilke ranch to attend the University of Arizona in Tucson. Harry lost touch with her during this time. But fate—as he would later recall—was soon about to enter the picture.

When Harry made a deal with Ada Mae's father, W.W. Wilke, to buy some new bulls for the Day ranch, the two men went to Big Spring, Texas, to look at the animals. On their return, they took the train back to El Paso. When they arrived, Ada Mae—home from college—was sitting in an automobile, waiting to drive them back to the ranch.

Harry and Ada Mae began a long-distance courtship, sending letters back and forth between the Day ranch and El Paso, where Ada Mae lived. By now, both considered themselves to be city people. Ada Mae had spent the last several years of her life in Tucson and El Paso, and Harry had just moved back to the ranch from Pasadena. Finally, in September 1928, tired of the distance separating them, they ran away to get married. O'Connor later recalled, "My father likes to say he met my mother when he went to buy some bulls from her father and she was part of the deal. That is not true, of course."[1]

The newlyweds set up housekeeping at the ranch. A year and a half later, baby Sandra was born. It was a hectic time. On the day of Sandra's birth—March 26, 1930—Ada Mae was in El Paso, where she had gone to have the baby. Harry was in a courtroom in distant Tucson, arguing in a federal suit involving a dispute with a former partner over the future of the Day ranch.

Adding to their problems was the thought of living so far from civilization with a brand-new baby to care for. They would be bringing their new daughter back to a four-room home with no running water, no electricity, no gas, and four herdsmen sleeping on the front porch. Harry considered moving to El Paso for a time. He finally made up his mind. The family would make a go of it on the ranch—just as Henry's family had done before him. Now all he had to do was convince his wife that it would be best for everyone.

"I thought, if other people could do it, I was sure I could," said Harry. "I just liked the wide open life."[2]

Ada Mae agreed. "I missed Harry, and the cowboys needed me," she said. "I had to love him, or think I did, to move out [to the ranch]."[3]

So in 1930, young Sandra Day moved into the family ranch started by Harry's father and began life on the wide-open prairies of Arizona. Harry was determined that his daughter would learn to ride and rope and shoot as well as any man. Sandra's mother stressed the importance of educating her daughter about the culture and social graces of the larger world that existed beyond ranch boundaries.

Following a hard day of work outdoors, Ada Mae would read to young Sandra. From early childhood, Sandra listened to stories her mother read from Book of the Month Club books, articles from the *Saturday Evening Post* and *National Geographic*, and encyclopedic entries from the *Book of Knowledge*.

For news, the Day family relied upon the *Los Angeles Times*,

From early childhood, O'Connor's mother read to her. Although her father wanted her to be an able ranch hand, Mrs. Day insisted that Sandra receive a good education. It is largely due to this fact that O'Connor has been so successful in her life.

the *Wall Street Journal*, and *Time* magazine, which they received by mail. As she grew up, Sandra became fascinated by the life and career of Clare Boothe Luce, the wife of *Time* magazine editor Henry R. Luce.

Because the ranch was so remote, Sandra had no playmates during her early childhood. Instead, she spent time with ranch hands Bug Quinn and Claude Tippett and made friends with the Lazy B's horses, cows, and cats.

Meanwhile, Sandra's mother was busy teaching her daughter the fine points of being a well-rounded young woman. Harry, on the other hand, taught Sandra how to ride a horse, drive a pickup truck, shoot jackrabbits, repair fences, set out salt blocks, and care for sick livestock.

On Saturday evenings, the Days would hop in the family truck and drive over to the small hotel in nearby Lordsburg, where Harry and Ada Mae would dance and socialize while young Sandra was watched over by an attentive bellhop.

By 1937, the Days were doing well enough to build a separate bunkhouse for their herdsmen and install indoor plumbing in the main house. Still, times were hard across the nation. High temperatures and severe drought throughout the southern, central, and western states signaled the end of the agricultural boom in the United States. Millions of acres of once-fertile land became dry and parched. It was the worst drought in American history.

The Dust Bowl, as the central United States soon came to be called, left farmers and ranchers—no longer able to grow crops—without income. Thousands lost their farms and land in bank foreclosures. Many simply packed up and left, unable to make a living from the land. They moved farther west or north to seek a better, more prosperous way of life.

"I was scared," Harry remembered. "I kept five hundred

dollars in a safe-deposit box in case we had to leave [the ranch]."[4]

Finally, the federal government introduced a program that paid ranchers twelve dollars apiece for dying cattle and twenty dollars a head for those worth shipping to market. It was less than the Days had been receiving for their cattle before the drought struck, but it was enough to help them keep their heads above water. It was enough to help them survive.

The Early Years

Young Sandra Day began school in 1935. Her mother told her that she would have to move to El Paso and live with her grandparents, the Wilkes. Sandra was an extremely bright child, and the schooling available near the ranch was limited. In El Paso, the educational opportunities were much greater. There, Sandra would receive the best education possible. The move would place her in class with her good friend—her cousin Flournoy Davis.

Sandra and Flournoy attended kindergarten and then went into first and second grade together at Crockett Public School. Following that, they transferred to Radford for third grade. Radford was an all-girls' school founded in 1910 as the El Paso School for Girls. It offered small classes of eight to ten students each. Sandra and Flournoy were soon inseparable friends. They ate with the other girls at school in a dining room, where a different teacher led discussions at each table.

Sandra's teachers soon recognized their student's intelligence and advanced her one grade. One teacher in particular stood out in Sandra's mind. Her name was Miss Fireoved. She taught public speaking—a skill Sandra would find useful later in life.

Frequently, the girls would be assigned a topic to discuss immediately after lunch, so that they were forced to learn to speak spontaneously, with no advance preparation. Sandra would practice her opening line to herself for hours on end. "Dr. Templin, faculty, and fellow students . . ."[1]

Dr. Templin was the headmistress of the school. She expected all of her students to learn not only their subjects, but also good manners. At least once a year, each student would be invited to lunch with Dr. Templin to show her progress. When it was time to speak, the student would pick a slip of paper with a topic she was expected to discuss.

During the summers, Sandra and Flournoy returned to the ranch, where they put on various productions. They used dried gourds for tea settings and put on plays for the cowboys on the bunkhouse porch.

The two rode daily, usually bareback. Often, they would gallop down to the old swimming hole, where they fished with safety-pin hooks and string for fishing line. They also enjoyed riding down to the Gila River, where Native Americans long since vanished from the area had left ancient pictures, called hieroglyphs, painted on the rock walls.

The girls learned from Harry how to shoot a .22-gauge rifle to rid the ranch of pesky jackrabbits, prairie dogs, rattlesnakes, and Gila monsters. From Ada Mae, they learned how to cook large, elaborate meals for company, as was the Day family custom at Thanksgiving and Christmas. They also learned how to shop from mail-order catalogs.

The good education Sandra received as a child, particularly in public speaking, was an important part of the road that led her to the Supreme Court.

When Sandra turned eight, her mother had another daughter, Ann. Two years later, she had a son, Alan. Although both children were too young to be playmates to Sandra, the three children got along well together. For Sandra, the hardest part about having a brother and sister was having to leave them for school.

As Sandra grew older, the Day family spent fewer and fewer summers on the ranch and more time traveling. They took a trip to Alaska, sailed a banana boat to Cuba and Honduras, went fishing in Mexico, and stayed at a beach house in California.

Through it all, Sandra's parents remained the most important influence on her life. From her mother, she learned to be gracious and dignified, even under trying conditions. From her father, she learned common sense, honesty, and fair play, as well as the ability to be self-sufficient.

As Sandra continued to advance through grade school, she found that each year away from the ranch made her more lonely, more homesick. Her father knew she felt "sad every time she had to leave home and go off to school," but there was nothing he could do about it.[2] It was in his daughter's best interest.

When Sandra was ready to begin eighth grade, Harry and Ada Mae decided they'd had enough separation of their family—at least for a while. They enrolled their daughter at the local school in Lordsburg. Even though the school was more than thirty miles from the ranch and required that she be bused both morning and evening, at least she would be living and sleeping at home again. But the memory of all those hours spent traveling on buses to and from school would leave a marked imprint in her memory. It would affect her feelings about the controversial issue of forced busing for years to come.

Following her grade-school graduation, Sandra entered high school. But she found the Lordsburg High School curriculum to be limited and soon transferred to Austin High School in El Paso. During her years there, she lost her childhood pudginess and grew tall and attractive. She also became an excellent student who made top grades.

"Sandra always knew how to handle herself," according to her high-school friend, Hondey Hill McAlmon.[3]

Upon graduating from high school, Sandra applied to Stanford University in California. She was the only graduating senior going to college that year. She had selected Stanford because of its reputation for academic excellence. She was so confident of being accepted, she never once considered applying to any other college.

But Sandra had several things working against her acceptance by Stanford. First, she was only sixteen years of age—not eighteen—because of having skipped two school grades. Second, she had never been given a college entrance exam by her Austin High School counselors. Third, she was female. In 1946, when thousands of American soldiers were returning from Europe following the end of World War II, few colleges were giving preference to young women.

Sandra's excellent academic record and her long list of extracurricular activities caught the eye of university officials, though. She also impressed the counselors when she appeared for a personal interview. She was as poised and serious about obtaining an education from Stanford as any other applicant. She was quickly accepted to the university, and when fall came, her parents drove her to registration. "We took her up there . . . deposited money in the Bank of America, and taught her how to write a check," her father said.[4]

At first, Sandra was afraid that she would feel isolated and homesick, as she'd felt when she was attending grade school in El Paso. Instead, she relished her new academic environment and looked forward to the years that lay ahead of her.[5]

As it would turn out, they would be years well spent.

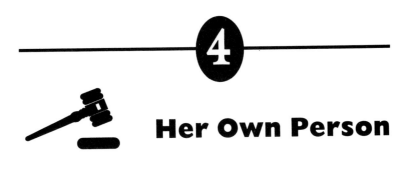

4

Her Own Person

In many ways, attending law school is similar to arguing a case in a courtroom. Both require the student or lawyer to come well prepared and to be ready to think quickly.

Sandra Day did just that. At Stanford, she prepared for her classes diligently. She studied long and hard, quickly becoming one of her teachers' favorite students. Before long, she was elected to the Order of the Coif. This was an honorary legal society whose membership carried a great deal of prestige with students and faculty alike. She was also named an editor of the *Stanford Law Review*.

Her work as an editor paid off. While at the *Review*, her job included reading articles submitted by professors and practicing lawyers. She spent countless hours in the library editing manuscripts and checking articles for facts. This taught her the importance of meticulous preparation and thorough research.

Working for the *Review* also brought Sandra Day prestige. It also afforded her the opportunity of a lifetime. One evening, while checking facts at the library for an upcoming article, she met another student editor who was working for the *Review* on the same piece. John Jay O'Connor, III, introduced himself and, after chatting for a while, asked Sandra Day out to dinner. She accepted. It was the first of many such dates over the next two years. Sandra even brought John to her home to meet her family back at the Lazy B.

"We liked John," Harry once joked about his future son-in-law, "but I've seen better cowboys."[1]

In June 1952, Sandra Day graduated from Stanford Law School. Her class ranking was third—higher than all but two other members of her graduating class. One of the students who ranked above her turned out to be William H. Rehnquist, a young lawyer-to-be who would eventually become Chief Justice of the United States Supreme Court.

On December 20, 1952, only six months after her graduation, Sandra Day married John O'Connor. They held a reception for more than two hundred guests at the Lazy B. John returned to Stanford to complete his final semester of school while Sandra began looking for a job.

Despite her academic excellence in law school, she had difficulty finding employment.

"I interviewed with law firms in Los Angeles and San Francisco," she said, "but none had ever hired a woman before as a lawyer, and they were not prepared to do so."[2] Finally, she received an offer from the law firm of Gibson, Dunn & Crutcher in Los Angeles. But it was not as a lawyer. Rather, the firm wanted to hire her as a legal secretary. As fate would have it, one of the firm's partners was a man named William French Smith, who would one day become attorney general of the United States and advise President Reagan to appoint Sandra Day O'Connor to the Supreme Court.

But O'Connor was not yet ready to settle for a secretarial job—not after all her hard work at Stanford. So she kept looking for employment as an attorney. Finally, she found a position as a law clerk in the office of the San Mateo, California, county attorney. She went to work there and quickly fell in love with the job. She learned early that her wide range of duties in public employment offered her more responsibility and a broader knowledge of law than she ever could have gotten working for a private law firm.

The following year, after graduating from Stanford, John O'Connor was appointed an officer in the United States Army and assigned to the Judge Advocate General's Corps (the army's legal division). He was transferred to Frankfurt, West Germany, and Sandra went with him. There, she found employment as a civilian lawyer for the Quartermaster Corps, which sold surplus supplies and bought food and equipment for the military. It was O'Connor's job to review military contracts and deal with any legal problems arising from the purchases and sales.

The O'Connors spent their free time in Europe traveling and skiing. They visited a total of fourteen countries, toured numerous museums and cathedrals, and skied in the Austrian Alps. John's tour of duty ended in December 1956, and the O'Connors moved back to the States. They bought some land and built a house in Phoenix, Arizona. Both took the Arizona bar exam and were admitted to practice law there. John took a job with Fennemore, Craig, von Ammon, and Udall. Sandra took enough time out from practicing law to give birth to the couple's first child, Scott Hampton O'Connor.

O'Connor enjoyed life as a new mother, but she wanted

to keep active in law. She went to work as an attorney at a new law firm in nearby Maryvale. There she worked mornings with lawyer Tom Tobin and spent her afternoons raising her child. As a lawyer, she wrote wills, reviewed landlord-tenant leases, and defended people who had been accused of drunk driving or theft. Her most important work, however, was defending clients who were too poor to pay for legal representation.

"I don't think any legal service for which I was paid gave me as much satisfaction as helping someone who needed it," she once told a reporter.[3]

When O'Connor gave birth to her second son, Brian, in January 1960, she stopped practicing law and concentrated on raising her family. Two years later, she gave birth to a third son, Jay—the couple's last. She would remain home for three more years before returning to public life as an attorney.

"Marriage is far more than an exchange of vows," she once observed. "It is the foundation of the family. . . . It is the relationship between ourselves and the generations that follow."[4]

Still, O'Connor maintained her contacts in the legal world through various types of volunteer work. She organized a lawyer-referral program for the county's bar association, took assignments as a trustee in bankruptcy estates, and served as a juvenile-court referee.

She also worked at the local YMCA and the Phoenix Historical Society. She played an active role in the community in which she lived. She joined the Republican party and began working in local political campaigns. Her husband and three growing boys placed demands upon her. Still, she found time to serve as a county precinct committee member from 1960 to 1964. She became a legislative district chairperson

Family has always been an important part of O'Connor's life. She even spent time working for the Governor's Commission on Marriage and the Family. She is pictured here with her husband, John, and their three sons.

from 1962 to 1965 and served as the vice-chairperson for the Maricopa County Republican Committee in 1964. She also spent time working for the Maricopa Board of Adjustments and Appeals, the Governor's Commission on Marriage and the Family, and the Arizona State Personnel Commission.

In 1965, O'Connor decided it was time to return to work as a lawyer. "I decided I should go back to paid employment to get a little peace and quiet in my life, so I went out and looked for a job," she joked with friends.[5] She called the office of the Arizona attorney general and was hired part-time as a state assistant attorney general. As her children grew older, she gradually took on more responsibilities outside the home. Within a year, she was once again working full-time, while remaining active in Republican politics.

Finally, in 1966, O'Connor's hard work and dedication to service paid off. The state senator from the O'Connors' district left the Arizona state legislature to take a position in the administration of President Richard M. Nixon. The head of the Arizona Republican party offered the recently vacated post to one of the party's most dedicated and hard-working members—Sandra Day O'Connor.

It was the right time for O'Connor to be entering politics. With the women's movement awakening the nation to the vast resources offered by women everywhere, O'Connor seemed to be the right woman at the right time. The Republican party had won a majority in both the state senate and house—the first time in Arizona's history. After being in the minority for so long, the Republicans were suddenly anxious to make changes in the way the state was being run.

O'Connor and other state senators began writing a tough new anti-smog law. They also revised the state's Liquor Control Board, wrote a new ethics law, and revised the state's property evaluation and assessment procedures. O'Connor soon earned a reputation for being a perfectionist in drafting bills and having the facts to support them at her fingertips. All this was due to her superb legal training and dedication to hard work.

"During the time the legislature is in session," she once told a reporter, "I devote my whole life to it."[6]

A year after her appointment to the state senate, O'Connor ran for reelection and won. Two years later, she won again. That same year, 1972, she was nominated as a state cochairperson for the Committee to Re-elect President Nixon and went to work campaigning for the party's number-one candidate. Meanwhile, she continued supporting those state issues she viewed as "good government"—laws opening up government meetings to the public, laws designed to help the mentally handicapped, and laws selecting judges for the state's Superior Court on the basis of merit and not political influence.

She seemed conservative at times, as she did when she voted against gun control and forced busing. At other times, she voted with the liberals—supporting a family planning bill and guaranteeing reporters the right to protect their news sources as confidential. In reality, she was more independent than either liberal or conservative. She would study a law or proposal, the facts and history behind it, the arguments both pro and con, and then make up her own mind as to whether or not she would support it—regardless of how others voted.

Because she was not expected to vote one way or the other, O'Connor was able to support a wide variety of bills, including bilingual education for Arizona's large Latino (Spanish-speaking) community and an on-the-job accident insurance program for migrant, or traveling, workers. She helped launch action to modernize the state's divorce laws and voted to restrict sulphur dioxide pollutants from local smelting operations. She took the unpopular stand of opposing public aid for private schools, even though she was on the board of directors of the private Phoenix Country Day School. She also drafted a bill that helped reinstate the death penalty in Arizona.

Through hard work, long hours, and exhaustive research, O'Connor soon distinguished herself as a superior leader. *Time* magazine praised her performance, and many of her colleagues on the floor—Republicans and Democrats alike—echoed the sentiments. Her hard work paid off once again when, shortly after the November 1972 national elections, eighteen Republican state senators met secretly to elect a new senate majority leader. Their choice: Sandra Day O'Connor. It was the first time in United States history that a woman had been named to that position.

Not everyone was pleased with the new senate majority leader's work in the legislature. One angry colleague was upset because O'Connor had blocked his pet project from reaching the senate floor for a vote. "If you were a man," he scolded, "I'd punch you in the mouth."

O'Connor, always quick on her feet and ready to meet any challenge, replied, "If you were a man, you could."[7]

O'Connor's mixed bag of conservatism and liberalism led Phoenix attorney David Tierney to remark that she was a "middle-roader—not an extreme rightist or an extreme leftist."[8]

Even when it came time to take a position on abortion—the most controversial topic during the early 1970s—O'Connor refused to adopt the views of her own party. Instead, she promoted her own. She supported one bill that limited Arizona state funds for abortions for women who could not afford to pay for them. She backed another bill that gave hospital workers the right to refuse to participate in abortions. This made the right-to-life movement—those who oppose abortions—happy.

Nearly in the same breath, however, she supported a bill that would have made family-planning information and methods (such as contraceptive devices and birth-control pills) available to anyone who wanted them. She angered conservative members of her own political party and delighted liberals by supporting the passage of the Equal Rights Amendment (ERA) for women. The amendment as proposed to the Constitution read, "Equality of rights under the law shall not be denied or abridged by the United States or by any state on account of sex."[9]

Two years later, O'Connor withdrew her support for the amendment, convinced that equality for women could be gained through other already-existing methods. This was just another example of Sandra Day O'Connor being her own person.

O'Connor quietly went about the business of securing rights for women in other less-public ways. She worked to change state laws concerning community property (property owned jointly by both a wife and her husband). Until the early 1970s, Arizona law had given all power to control community property to the husband. O'Connor helped change the situation by carefully building into a law on marriage and divorce a section offering husbands and wives joint control of community property. The law passed without any opposition.

She also was instrumental in changing a state law that prohibited women from working more than a forty-hour week. This limited the income-earning potential of women.

Yet, despite her support for laws that gave women greater equality, O'Connor never lost sight of her support for the traditional values of motherhood and family. During the height of the women's movement in 1970, O'Connor addressed a group of Arizona high-school students. She only half-jokingly said, "I come to you tonight wearing my bra and my wedding band."[10] It was a clear reference to her support for the differing roles of men and women in society.

Another frequent theme in O'Connor's talks before various groups was the importance of the individual in American society. The nature of society, she emphasized, was built around individuals who become involved. She urged her listeners to learn the "vehicles of power in and out of government and how to influence them."[11]

As the years passed, O'Connor gained greater influence in Arizona state politics. She also gained a greater understanding of the importance of the way state government works. Years later, she would come to understand that, while the federal government plays an important role in the lives of all Americans, the states make possible one of the most valuable liberties of all—the right of the people to govern themselves.

Judge Sandra Day O'Connor

In 1974, O'Connor announced that she would not seek a third term as a state senator. She had decided the time was right to leave politics. She would return to what she loved best—the law.

She campaigned hard for the position of trial judge on the Maricopa County Superior Court. She appealed to Phoenix-area residents who had had enough of the rampant crime in their city. She won easily, defeating a judge already occupying the office in the process.

As the city's newest judge, O'Connor presided over trials, instructed juries on their rights and obligations, imposed sentences in criminal cases, and did all the things a trial judge is required to do. Within a matter of months, O'Connor had heard nearly all the issues that a judge can hear—from divorce to dealing drugs to murder. She soon gained a reputation as a

In 1974, O'Connor was elected as a judge to the Maricopa County Superior Court. She held this position for nearly five years until she was nominated to the Arizona Court of Appeals, where she heard cases for eighteen months.

formidable—and sometimes feared—judge. She let the attorneys in her courtroom know that she expected them to arrive in court well prepared and to be knowledgeable defenders of their clients' rights. She also expected them to be as hard working as she was, which—considering her relentless pursuit of the law—sometimes proved difficult.

On occasion, O'Connor even went so far as to advise criminal defendants to fire their ill-prepared lawyers and hire better ones. She showed little tolerance for lawyers who took the law lightly.

Phoenix attorney Alice Bendheim, who had helped O'Connor revise Arizona's community-property laws, said, "You didn't want to go in there [to the courtroom] if you weren't prepared . . . She did not appreciate having her time wasted."[1]

Although she had a sense of humor, O'Connor showed little inclination to smile while on the bench. But if an attorney appeared well prepared and ready to get down to business, she proved herself a fair, persuadable, and open-minded judge.

During the next four years, O'Connor gained statewide notoriety for her competence and fairness on the bench. In 1978, United States Senator Barry Goldwater and the Arizona Republican party invited her to run for governor against Democrat Bruce Babbitt. O'Connor reluctantly refused, deciding instead to remain on the Superior Court bench, where she felt she could do the most good.

Babbitt was elected governor in November. Eleven months later, he nominated O'Connor to the Arizona Court of Appeals. She was quickly confirmed to the position.

O'Connor's duties as an appeals judge were different from

what they had been as a trial judge. She worked alone as a trial judge. Now she found herself presiding over cases in which three judges worked together towards a decision. Instead of deciding such day-to-day questions as guilt and innocence, she now found herself contemplating broader questions of law and principle. She no longer decided whether or not a person accused of murder was actually guilty. She instead found herself ruling on the subtle legal differences between second-degree murder and manslaughter and on whether or not the evidence used in the original trial was obtained legally.

The format of the appeals-court cases was also different from what O'Connor had experienced as a trial judge. Instead of listening to witnesses and deciding guilt or innocence, an appeals-court judge hears oral arguments in which lawyers for each side present their views on whatever law is in question. The judge then adjourns to consider the case and to review prior cases, statutes, and written materials submitted by the lawyers. Finally, the judge reaches a decision and writes his or her opinion on the case.

On a three-judge panel, each of the judges gets one vote. The majority of judges rules, and the opinion they reach is written for the court records. If any judge dissents, or disagrees with the majority opinion, that judge has the right to write a dissenting opinion explaining how his or her view differs from the majority's.

During her eighteen months of service as an appeals-court judge, O'Connor published twenty-nine opinions, most dealt with routine issues such as workers' compensation, landlord-tenant relations, and some criminal matters. She also appeared regularly as a guest speaker.

> I used to be very nervous about public appearances. . . .
> I would be shaking, even my head. I was terrified
> even when I got married, the first time in court as a
> lawyer, the first time I sat on the bench as a trial
> judge.
>
> One of the wonderful things about growing older is
> that you get over your terror. It is a fabulous blessing
> of advancing age. The more you do something, the
> easier it gets . . . [2]

Her performance was regularly reviewed by the Arizona
State Bar Association, which gave her top ratings for her
thoroughness and meticulously written opinions. Not
surprisingly, the bar—made up of Arizona lawyers—gave her
slightly lower ratings on her dealings with attorneys. This was
due to the fact that some of the lawyers objected to her no-
nonsense approach.

O'Connor took comfort in both appraisals. She was
pleased that her peers found her to be well prepared and
knowledgeable. She was somewhat disappointed that they
found fault with her high expectations of their courtroom
performance. But she felt that their failure to live up to her
expectations was their problem and not hers. She was not
about to lower her courtroom standards merely to increase her
popularity with her fellow attorneys. [3]

As the months passed for Sandra Day O'Connor as an
appellate court judge, she continued to perform the best way
she knew how, regardless of whose toes she stepped on. For
most attorneys, a career capped by a state appellate judgeship
would have been enough to satisfy them for a lifetime.

As it was for O'Connor for a long while, at least. She had

been satisfied with prospect of living out the rest of her life in the family's adobe house on the desert, where she and her husband had friends and led a comfortable way of life.

On July 7, 1981, however, President Reagan announced that he was nominating her to fill a vacancy on the United States Supreme Court. Her life—and the lives of all Americans— was about to change forever.

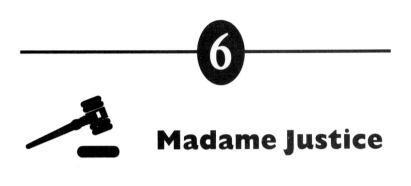

Madame Justice

Sandra Day O'Connor did not walk into the Senate Judiciary Committee hearings unprepared. Never before had she been through anything like this, but she had seen the hearings on television. She also had met for several days with Justice Department officials, who had briefed her on questions she was likely to receive.

Still, she could not have imagined what the opening day of hearings would be like. As she strode through the door of the Senate Office Building, Senate committee chairman Strom Thurmond escorted her on his arm. Committee members, aware of the historical opportunity confronting them, rushed forward to shake her hand.

O'Connor took her seat before the committee. In an introductory remark, she talked of the importance of marriage and family life. She introduced her husband, John, and their sons to the committee members, and then the proceedings began. O'Connor told the committee members, "I happily share the honor [of being nominated to the U.S. Supreme Court] with millions of American women of yesterday and today whose abilities and whose conduct have given me this opportunity for service."[1]

With right-to-life demonstrators marching outside the building, the committee members queried O'Connor about her position on abortion. They asked her about several votes she had cast while in the Arizona state legislature. In 1970, she had supported the repeal of a state law that made abortion a criminal act. Did that mean, the senators wanted to know, that O'Connor favored the legalization of abortion?

O'Connor explained that she had voted against the Arizona law because she felt it was too vague to be effective.

The members of the committee then asked O'Connor if she was against abortion and if she would work toward reversing the 1973 Supreme Court decision of *Roe* v. *Wade*, which made abortion under most circumstances legal.

O'Connor replied that, while she was personally opposed to abortion, she didn't feel it was the right of the Court to decide the abortion issue. That was, she insisted, the obligation of the legislature.

"I know well the difference between a legislator and a judge, and the role of the judge is to interpret the law, not make it," she said.[2] The remark immediately won favor with some of the committee's legislators.

Over and over the members queried O'Connor on *Roe* v. *Wade* and how she would vote on future abortion issues that might come before the Court. Each time, she stated that she could not discuss such matters for fear of being guilty of prejudging a case.

One Republican senator, Jeremiah Denton of Alabama,

was growing frustrated. After grilling O'Connor on the subject of abortion for half an hour, he still hadn't gotten an answer that satisfied him. When the committee chairman asked Denton if he wanted another fifteen minutes for questioning, the senator waved him off. "I don't know whether another month would do."[3]

Following the three-day hearing, an article in *Newsweek* magazine said that O'Connor had followed the "three rules of conduct for a successful justice-to-be: It's better to be seen than heard, speak only when spoken to, and try not to discuss religion or politics."[4]

O'Connor herself told one reporter who had asked if she found the hearings unnerving, "I really wasn't nervous. I found the proceedings very fascinating."[5]

The Senate committee members voted 17 to 0 to confirm O'Connor. Denton abstained. A week after the hearings, the full Senate confirmed O'Connor's appointment by a vote of 99 to 0.

Following her approval, Vice-President George Bush and a crowd of cheering supporters greeted the first woman Justice on the steps of the Capitol. Later that day, O'Connor, in addressing a banquet held in her honor, said, "Thomas Jefferson and James Madison would be turning over in their graves right now, but let's hope Abigail Adams [an early fighter for women's rights] would be pleased."[6]

The following Monday, Justice Sandra Day O'Connor went to work at the sprawling, marble-columned Supreme Court building. There to greet her were hundreds of congratulatory letters—just the beginning of more then four thousand such letters she would eventually receive and acknowledge within the days following her appointment to the Court.

"It's been touching to see how women of all ages have responded to the appointment of a woman to the Court . . .,"[7] O'Connor said.

On September 29, O'Connor began preparing for the Court's opening session, which was scheduled for Monday, October 5. Before her were more than one thousand petitions received over the summer from litigants who wanted the Supreme Court to hear their cases. The Justices would meet in closed-door conferences to determine which cases would be chosen for hearings and which left undisturbed. Of the approximately five thousand petitions the Court received that year, only about one hundred fifty were selected by the Court for argument.

The decision of which cases the Court hears is determined by vote. A minimum of four votes in favor of a hearing—also called a review—must be received before a case will be accepted by the Court. Only then will new arguments in the case be heard.

So on October 5, precisely at 10 A.M., the red velvet curtain behind the great mahogany bench opened and all nine Justices entered the Courtroom and took their seats. Then the marshal announced the traditional opening to the session with the same words that have been used since the Court's first session in 1789:

> Oyez, oyez, oyez. All persons having business before the honorable, the Supreme Court of the United States, are admonished to draw near and give their attention, for the Court is now sitting. God save the United States and this Honorable Court. [The word, Oyez, pronounced OH-yay or OH-yes, means "Hear ye" and is used to call order to the Court.][8]

So began the new career of Justice Sandra Day O'Connor.

Placing her left hand on both her family Bible and the marshal's Bible that her husband held, Sandra Day O'Connor was sworn in as a Supreme Court Justice by the Chief Justice Warren E. Burger.

While it took some time for her to get used to Supreme Court traditions and its method of operation, she caught on quickly and was soon writing opinions that her peers found both exciting and insightful.

O'Connor's first assignment was to write the majority opinion for *Watt* v. *Energy Action.* The case had been relatively simple. All nine Justices agreed that United States Secretary James Watt had acted constitutionally in administering the Outer Continental Shelf Lands Act Amendments. The amendments were designed to help preserve the environ- ment. The Justices ruled that Energy Action Educational Foundation could not sue Watt because they had not suffered an "injury" as a result of Watt's actions.

Next, O'Connor was asked to write the opinion for *Rose* v. *Lundy.* In this case, a man named Lundy had sued for release from a state prison, saying that his constitutional rights had been violated during his trial. This was a much more complicated case than the last, involving the *writ of habeas corpus.* The Great Writ, which it is sometimes called, offers a means by which prison inmates can be freed if they can prove that their federal constitutional rights were violated.

But the Court ruled 8 to 1 against Lundy because it found that he had not fully explored all remedies available in the state courts. Called the "total exhaustion" rule, the legal concept holds that an individual must use up, or "exhaust," all possibilities available in the lower courts before bringing a case before the United States Supreme Court.

This opinion gave O'Connor an opportunity to emphasize her belief in the states' lower-court system. The case turned out to be difficult, talking five months before the Justices agreed on an opinion. Even then, the majority was divided as to why they voted as they did. Some Justices agreed with O'Connor's opinion, while others found fault with it and chose to write their own concurring opinions.

O'Connor wrote two other opinions in her first year on the bench. In both *Engle* v. *Isaac* and *United States* v. *Frady,* O'Connor expanded her views on the *writ of habeas corpus.* In both decisions, the Court agreed to make it more difficult for a prisoner to win the right to a new trial, a different sentence, or total freedom because a lower court had violated his or her constitutional rights. It was part of a conservative movement that supported the arguments of the police, prosecutors, and state judges over those of defendants.

A majority of Justices supported both opinions, and O'Connor soon began making a name for herself. She became a knowledgeable voice in matters dealing with the limitation of prisoners' access to federal courts. She also was building a reputation as a conservative Justice who strongly supported the return of power and responsibility to state and local officials.

Not all of O'Connor's opinions were popular, of course. In 1982, the court voted on a case in which a Long Island, New York, school board removed nine books from the school library because they were viewed as offensive. The books included such classics as Kurt Vonnegut's *Slaughterhouse Five,* Eldridge Cleaver's *Soul on Ice,* and Richard Wright's *Black Boy.* In response, students at the Island Trees Union Free School sued the board.

The Court voted 5 to 4 in favor of the students, claiming that the removal of the books was the equivalent of censorship, which in most instances is banned by the United States Constitution. O'Connor was one of the dissenting Justices. In her opinion, she wrote, "If the school board can set the curriculum, select teachers, and determine initially what books to purchase for the school library, it surely can decide which books to discontinue or remove from the school library so long as it does not also interfere with the right of students to read the material and to discuss it."[9]

The following year, another free-speech case came before the local courts when the principal of a Hazelwood, Missouri, high school ordered two pages deleted from the student newspaper. He insisted that articles about divorce and student pregnancy were inappropriate and should therefore not be published in the school paper.

Student editors of the newspaper, which was published as part of the school's journalism program, sued the school. When the case finally reached the Supreme Court in 1988, O'Connor joined the majority of Justices in ruling with the school. Her reason was that public school officials have broad powers to restrict school publications, plays, and other school-sponsored activities, and these powers, according to the Justices, extend to student publications.

During her first two years on the bench, one of the most persistent issues to appear before the Court was that of religion in public life. As early as 1968, the Supreme Court had struck down an Arkansas law that forbade the teaching of evolution in public institutions. In 1980, it ruled that a Kentucky law requiring the posting of the Ten Commandments in each public school classroom was unconstitutional. Both decisions were based upon a constitutional guarantee of the separation of church (religious beliefs) and state (public places, such as public schools, libraries, hospitals, etc.).

In 1982, O'Connor was forced to carefully form her thoughts on the separation of church and state. In *United States* v. *Lee*, the Amish, a religious group, asked the Court to grant them a free exercise exemption from paying social security taxes. Fearing an ocean of lawsuits by people seeking to avoid paying taxes because of religious beliefs, the Court found the government's interest in denying the Amish an exemption to be compelling. This meant that the government's argument was solid enough to win the case. O'Connor voted with the majority.

O'Connor had spent much time researching the pros and cons of the Amish request. Little did she realize, however, that right around the corner lay several other more difficult cases awaiting her attention.

In 1983, the lower courts had ruled that a nativity scene in Pawtucket, Rhode Island, violated the Constitution's First Amendment by endorsing a Christian symbol. This violated the separation of church and state. In this case, *Lynch* v. *Donnelly*, the Supreme Court was asked to review the lower court's decision.

The case involved the city of Pawtucket, which owned and each year erected a Christmas display in its main shopping district. The display included a wide variety of Christmas symbols, including a Santa's house, a Christmas tree, various cut-out animal figures, colored Christmas-tree lights, and a full-size nativity scene depicting the birth of Jesus.

The plaintiffs in the case, who were all Pawtucket residents, claimed that the presence of the nativity scene in the display amounted to the city's endorsement of Christianity. That, they said, violated the establishment clause of the First Amendment to the Constitution of the United States, which guarantees the separation of church and state.

On March 5, 1984, Chief Justice Warren Burger, writing for a majority of five Justices, pointed out that the Christmas display included many nonreligious figures as well as religious ones. These included candy canes, figures of carolers, and a Santa Claus house. The purpose of the display, he said, was not to promote religion in public but rather to express "a friendly community spirit of good will in keeping with the season."[10]

Even the nativity scene, he said, served no other purpose than to depict the historical origins of the Christmas holiday.

Four Justices—William Brennan, Thurgood Marshall, Harry Blackmun, and John Stevens—dissented. They believed that the nativity scene's "effect on minority religious groups, as well as on those who may reject all religion, is to convey the message that their views are not similarly worthy of public recognition nor entitled to public support."[11]

O'Connor joined with Burger and the majority, providing the necessary fifth vote for a decision. In a separate concurring [agreeing] opinion, she wrote that the nativity scene "does not communicate a message that the government intends to endorse . . . Christian beliefs." She went on to say that the display "celebrates a public holiday, and no one contends that the declaration of that holiday is understood to be an endorsement of religion."[12]

The New York Times, in observing the Court's decision, noted that the ruling was the most important in years concerning the boundary between government and organized religion. It in effect signaled the willingness of the Court to play down the literal interpretation of the separation of church and state.

The following year, 1985, O'Connor concurred in the Court's 6 to 3 ruling against an Alabama law that had permitted a daily one-minute period of meditation or prayer in the state's public schools. The Court's ruling was geared to force the government to maintain a complete sense of neutrality where religion was concerned—neither encouraging nor discouraging it.

That same year, O'Connor voted with the majority in an

8 to 1 decision in *Thornton* v. *Caldor*. Donald E. Thornton, a Caldor™ department store manager in Connecticut, had told his employer that his religion forbade him to work on Sundays. A state law provided employees with the right not to work on their Sabbath. Store personnel, however, disagreed. They demoted Thornton to the position of clerk. Thornton sued and won his case in the Connecticut Superior Court. An appeal to the state supreme court was lost.

Finally, Thornton took the case to the United States Supreme Court, which ruled in favor of the store. The Court held that the state law violated the Establishment Clause of the First Amendment. Religious laws, according to the majority opinion, were unconstitutional, since the government "must take pains not to compel people to act in the name of any religion."[13]

During her first eight years on the Court, O'Connor wrote opinions on a wide variety of cases—from court procedure, copyright, criminal confessions, race, employment, and immigration to oil drilling off the California coast, land reform in Hawaii, and the licensing of nuclear-power plants. But of all the decisions, those given the most notoriety by the press were the ones associated with abortion.

The first case to test O'Connor's position on abortion came in November 1983, when oral arguments were heard in the case *Akron* v. *Akron Center for Reproductive Health, Inc.* The case involved the city of Akron, Ohio, which had placed a number of restrictions on performing abortions in the second trimester, or second three months, of a woman's pregnancy. This seemed to some supporters of abortion to be in direct opposition to the Court's 1973 ruling in *Roe* v. *Wade*.

In effect, the city banned second-trimester abortions performed in clinics rather than in hospitals, imposed a requirement that physicians provide detailed information about abortions to women before they signed a consent form to have an abortion, and required a twenty-four-hour waiting period between giving consent and having an abortion performed.

In its 6 to 3 majority ruling, the Court found in favor of the Akron Center for Reproductive Health. It ruled that the city's requirement for hospitalization increased the cost of abortions without significantly increasing the woman's safety. It found that the information required to be given to the woman was written in such a way so as to persuade the woman not to have an abortion, rather than merely to inform her about the abortion process. It also ruled that the twenty-four-hour waiting period was unconstitutional.

O'Connor agreed with some members of the Court that at least a few of the points in *Roe* were likely to cause problems. She suggested that it was wrong to attempt to divide a pregnancy into three rigid trimesters and to forbid abortions after viability—or that time during pregnancy when a fetus could be expected to survive outside the mother's womb. Advancing medical technology was likely to push viability earlier and earlier into the pregnancy, thus eventually making the guidelines in *Roe* useless.

But the faults she found with *Roe* fell short of allowing her to support the majority decision in the case. She felt instead that the regulations imposed by the city were not excessive in light of the overall importance of the question of abortion. For her, neither the hospitalization nor the waiting period requirements imposed by the city were unduly restrictive. Abortions, after all, were already available in local hospitals, and the waiting period was "a small cost to impose to ensure that the woman's decision is well considered in light of its certain and irreparable consequences on fetal life. . . ."[14] O'Connor, along with Justices Rehnquist and White, dissented.

While *Akron* was the first of the abortion decisions in which O'Connor participated, the most important and wide reaching of her abortion rulings came in 1989 in *Webster* v. *Reproductive Health Services*. In this case, argued before the Court on April 29, the legality of a Missouri state law that placed a number of restrictions on abortion was being challenged.

Missouri's state constitution began with a preamble that said that life begins at conception. Although the Supreme Court had never ruled on when life begins (at conception, at birth, or somewhere in between), opponents of the Missouri restrictions argued that the statement conflicted with the Court's 1973 ruling in *Roe* v. *Wade*. It said that each state could adopt its own theory of when human life begins.

In *Webster*, a 5 to 4 majority of the Court disagreed. The majority opinion stated that, since there were no laws tied to the statement, the statement did not conflict with *Roe* and was therefore not unconstitutional.

Another restriction of the state's abortion rules banned the use of state property for conducting abortions. That meant that no Missouri public hospital could perform an abortion, whether it was paid for privately or with state funds.

The Court once again upheld the Missouri restriction, ruling that it was no different in effect than the ban on public funding of abortions, which the Court had earlier found to be constitutional in *Harris* v. *McRae*, 1980.

Finally, a third state restriction required physicians to perform medical tests to determine the viability of the fetus in cases where the fetus—in the doctor's judgment—was twenty weeks old or older. In *Roe*, twenty weeks falls with the second trimester, when states could prohibit abortions only to assure the health and safety of the mother.

Abortion has always been an important issue for O'Connor—from her interviews with the Senate Judiciary Committee (during which abortion protestors marched outside) to Supreme Court cases like *Akron* v. *Akron Center for Reproductive Health, Inc.* and *Webster* v. *Reproductive Health Services.*

O'Connor noted during the oral arguments that there is a four-week margin of error in trying to determine the age of a fetus. When a doctor believes that a fetus is twenty weeks old, it might actually be as old as twenty-four weeks. That would put the pregnancy in the third trimester. Under *Roe*, abortions are forbidden in the third trimester when, in the opinion of the doctor, the fetus is viable. Therefore, O'Connor pointed out, the Missouri restriction did not upset the findings in *Roe* and was not unconstitutional.

Chief Justice William H. Rehnquist went one step further, suggesting that the second trimester ruling in *Roe* should be overturned to more closely match the Missouri state restriction. O'Connor disagreed, preferring to leave the *Roe* trimester rules in place. This caused Justice Antonin Scalia to chastise her soundly. Scalia was one of three conservative Justices appointed to the bench by President Reagan. He was well known to favor the complete overturn of *Roe*. O'Connor, on the other hand, believed that the best way to deal with *Roe* was on a point-by-point and case-by-case basis.[15]

Nonetheless, with a majority of the Justices ruling in favor of Webster, the framework to overturn *Roe* v. *Wade* was laid. The states, it seemed, could adopt any regulations they chose to promote their interests in protecting the life of the fetus. They could possibly even go so far as to make the performing or obtaining of abortions illegal.

The majority claimed that the Court had not intended such wide-reaching implications, saying that it had confidence that state legislatures would not return to the "dark ages" of such restrictions on abortions.[16]

Justice Harry Blackmun, who had authored the decision of *Roe*, wrote a strong dissent to the majority ruling. Brennan, Marshall, and Stevens joined in, which seemed to show that the Court had come close to overruling *Roe.*

In its controversial decision, the Court had upheld the Missouri abortion law, declaring that the state could prohibit the performing of abortions in public hospitals, forbid the use of state funds for abortion counseling, and require doctors to refuse to perform abortions after the twentieth week of a healthy pregnancy. But the controversy surrounding the decision was not so much what the Court had ruled as it was what the Court had done. By supporting restrictions on abortion, it had reopened the political battle between pro- and antiabortion forces.

Abortion interest groups viewed *Webster* as an attack on *Roe.* Those in favor of increased restrictions on the availability of abortions used the decision to pressure state legislatures into taking a firmer antiabortion stand. Those against increased restrictions used the decision to gather unified support for pro-abortion advocates.

O'Connor, who had provided the necessary fifth vote to uphold the Missouri law, soon found herself the target of both liberals, who did not want the Court tampering with the abortion rights granted by *Roe,* and conservatives, who had hoped that O'Connor would use the opportunity to strike down *Roe* altogether. But O'Connor was not prepared to do so. She stated in her written opinion that state restrictions on abortion are permissible so long as they do not "impose an undue burden" on women seeking abortions.[17] She also repeated her belief in the right of the states to protect human life.

So the first eight years of O'Connor's role as a Supreme Court Justice were marked by controversy. Justices Antonin Scalia, Anthony Kennedy, William H. Rehnquist, and Byron R. White were considered conservative. Their opinions could often be determined in advance by their past voting records.

Justices Harry Blackmun, Thurgood Marshall, William J. Brennan, Jr., and John Paul Stevens III, on the other hand, were considered liberal. Their opinions could likewise often be determined by their past voting records.

The only Justice who did not fit the conservative/liberal mold was Sandra Day O'Connor. One reporter for *The New York Times* speculated that O'Connor was the only Justice not clearly on one side or the other—which is perhaps the best way for a Supreme Court Justice to be.

What no one could know at the time was that an even greater benchmark of O'Connor's independence was yet to come. In January 1989, she would go head to head with one of the most liberal Supreme Court Justices in the history of the United States.

For nearly all of his adult life, Thurgood Marshall had been a renowned civil-rights activist and constitutional expert. As a young attorney working for the National Association for the Advancement of Colored People (NAACP), he spear-headed the cause of classroom integration in the Supreme Court case of *Brown* v. *Board of Education of Topeka, Kansas.* He nearly single-handedly broke down the racial barriers at educational facilities throughout the South. He helped bring about the integration of the Armed Forces. He was, in short, the most successful civil-rights activist—promoting the cause of rights for minorities—in history.

In his long and distinguished career on the Court, Marshall held a unique interpretation of the United States Constitution. He viewed it as a living, changing document that helped to overturn the death penalty in *Furman* v. *Georgia,* protect the rights of a free press in *New York Times* v. *United States,* uphold women's rights to abortion in *Roe* v.

Wade, and limit presidential powers in *United States* v. *Nixon.*

When Sandra Day O'Connor joined the Court, Marshall—who had been the first African American ever appointed a Supreme Court Justice—had an ally. Marshall took her under his wing and helped guide her through her earliest and toughest days of transition from judge to Justice.

O'Connor was grateful. In a tribute to Marshall for the *Stanford Law Review,* she wrote:

> I have experienced gender discrimination, such as when law firms would only hire me, a "lady lawyer," as a legal secretary, to understand how one could seek to minimize interaction with those intolerant of difference. That Justice Marshall never hid from prejudice but thrust himself into its midst has been an encouragement and challenge to me. . . . [He was like] a man who sees the world exactly as it is and pushes on to make it what it can become. . . . No one could avoid being touched by his soul.[18]

Now, in January 1989, Sandra Day O'Connor found herself going head-to-head with fellow Justice Thurgood Marshall. Not in public, not in the press, but in the chambers and conference room of the Supreme Court building. It all began with the Court's hearing of *City of Richmond* v. *J. A. Croson Company.*

In 1989, the city of Richmond, Virginia, had an African-American population of more than 50 percent. It also had a poor record of hiring minority workers to do city jobs. In order to help make up for its minority-hiring record, the city decided to require that at least 30 percent of all of its contracts go to minority-construction businesses. That meant that, if Richmond scheduled ten million dollars' worth of construction in any given year, 30 percent of that amount, or three million dollars, would go to construction firms owned by or made up mostly of minorities. It was considered to be a positive step toward trying to remedy an age-old injustice.

But the white owners of a construction company, J. A. Croson, complained that the 30-percent quota was actually a form of "reverse discrimination." They sued the city of Richmond after the city cancelled a contract with Croson for failing to find enough black subcontractors to meet the city's new minority-hiring law.

When the case finally made its way to the Supreme Court and oral arguments were heard, the Court ruled that the Richmond law violated the right of white contractors to equal protection. The city had failed to establish past discrimination against qualified minorities in the local construction business. O'Connor agreed with the majority, writing, "Racial classifications are suspect, and that means that simple legislative assurances of good intention cannot suffice."[19]

O'Connor, after carefully considering the Richmond law, decided that racially linked spending quotas could be justified only if they served a "compelling state interest" by correcting "identified discrimination" by the government or by private companies. In other words, in order for the law to be constitutional, the discrimination had to be specific in nature and not general. In her opinion, the Richmond law failed the "specific" test.[20]

Justice Marshall, who had spent most of his life fighting for racial equality, wrote a strong dissent. Affirmative-action programs like the Richmond law, he believed, had to be judged by a flexible standard that takes into account the nation's long and shameful racial history. "In concluding that remedial classifications warrant no different standard . . . than the most brutal and repugnant forms of state-sponsored

61

Although Thurgood Marshall (shown here) took Sandra Day O'Connor under his wing when she became a Justice, their opinions clashed on the issue of racial quotas.

racism," he wrote, "a majority of this Court signals that it regards racial discrimination as largely a phenomenon of the past, and that government bodies need no longer preoccupy themselves with rectifying racial injustice."[21]

O'Connor disagreed, writing, "While there is no doubt that the sorry history of both private and public discrimination in this country has contributed to a lack of opportunities for black entrepreneurs [business owners], this observation, standing alone, cannot justify a rigid racial quota in the awarding of public contracts in Richmond, Virginia."[22]

Although Marshall was furious with the Court's decision, there was little he could do to reverse the steadily developing Court trend away from the use of racial quotas to make up for past discrimination.[23] He was saddened that his sister on the Court had persuaded a majority of its members to vote against him, but O'Connor was just as firm in her own beliefs.[24]

In reaching her decision, O'Connor had once again marked her career on the Court as an independent. In fact, she had gone so far as to take the supreme risk—pitting herself and her reputation against a legend in the American judiciary system. She had long ago proved to the world that she was nobody's pawn. Now it seemed she was determined to prove to the world that she was even more independent than it had suspected. Her reputation on the bench was firmly entrenched. She had become the Court's reigning maverick.

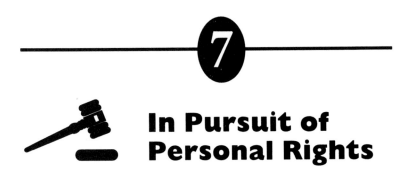

In Pursuit of Personal Rights

While O'Connor may be best known in public circles for her decisions on abortion, she also has presided over several controversial personal-liberties cases. The first such case concerned with protecting an individual's personal rights came in 1986 with the hearing of *Bowers* v. *Hardwick*.

Although the gay-rights movement had been alive in the United States for decades, it wasn't until the 1970s that a large number of gay Americans went public. They demanded rights that had been denied to them in the past—simply because they were not heterosexual. These demands placed the gay movement in the spotlight and brought new challenges before the nation's courts.

In 1982, Michael Hardwick was arrested in Atlanta, Georgia, while having sexual relations with another adult male in the bedroom of his own home. According to an 1816 Georgia state law, sodomy is illegal. The original American colonies all adopted laws that made the commission of sodomy a crime. All fifty states did likewise, and the laws remained on the books until 1960. By the time *Bowers* came before the Court, though, more than half the states had dropped their sodomy laws.

Georgia was not one of them. The penalty for sodomy there was twenty years in prison. The law applied equally to married or single persons, either heterosexual or homosexual.

For Michael Hardwick, his problems began outside a gay bar in Atlanta. A police officer ticketed him for drinking outside the bar. A few days later, Hardwick paid the fine, but there was a mix-up in the records department, and a warrant was issued for Hardwick's arrest. An officer went to Hardwick's home, opened the bedroom door, and saw Hardwick having sex with another male.

The officer arrested the two and charged them with sodomy. Following a preliminary hearing on the charge, the local district attorney declined to present the case to the grand jury without additional evidence. The charges were dropped, but Hardwick, with the help of the American Civil Liberties Union, sued the state's attorney general, Michael Bowers, in Federal District Court, challenging the constitutionality of the Georgia sodomy law as it applied to homosexual activity between two consenting adults in their own home.

The United States District Court dismissed the lawsuit. Hardwick then appealed to the United States Court of Appeals, which reinstated the suit. It also ruled that private sexual behavior among consenting adults was a fundamental right protected by the Ninth and Fourteenth Amendments of the Constitution. The Georgia district attorney was anxious to uphold the state's sodomy law and to overturn the lower court's ruling. He pointed out that appeals courts in

California and the District of Columbia had previously arrived at opposite judgments over the same facts. They petitioned the United States Supreme Court to hear the case. The Court granted a review, and oral arguments were scheduled to be heard in March 1986.

The state's case was presented by Assistant Attorney General Michael Hobbs, who began his oral argument:

> Mr. Chief Justice, and may it please the Court.
>
> This case presents the question of whether or not there is a fundamental right under the Constitution of the United States to engage in consensual private homosexual sodomy.
>
> It is our position that there is no fundamental right to engage in this conduct and that the state of Georgia should not be required to show a compelling state interest to prohibit this conduct . . .
>
> Many of the Court's decisions have followed the history and traditions of our nation in making its determination as to whether or not a particular activity is entitled to constitutional protection as a fundamental right. Thus far this Court has concluded that the right of privacy includes matters which involve marriage, the family, procreation, abortion, childrearing, and child education. It has never concluded, and I would suggest to the Court that there is no constitutional warrant to conclude, that there should be a fundamental right to engage in homosexual sodomy or any other type of extramarital sexual relationships.[1]

After opening his arguments with the historical basis for the state's law, Hobbs went on to bring up the moral aspects of sodomy.

Moral issues and social issues, it is submitted to the Court, should be decided by the people of this nation. Laws which are written concerning those issues or rescinded concerning those issues should be made by the representatives of those people. Otherwise, the natural order of the public debate and the formulation of consensus concerning these issues, it is submitted, would be interrupted and misshapen.

It is a right of the nation and of the states to maintain a decent society, representing the collective moral aspirations of the people. The Eleventh Circuit [the court that originally ruled in favor of Hardwick] and the respondents in this case, by failing to adhere to the traditions, the history, of this nation and the collective conscience of our people would remove from this area of legitimate state concern a most important function of government and possibly make each individual a law unto himself. It is submitted to this Court that this is not the balance that our forefathers intended between individual liberties and legitimate state legislative prerogatives.[2]

The Court then recognized Laurence Tribe, a Harvard law professor and the attorney for Hardwick, who opened his defense.

Mr. Chief Justice, and may it please the Court.

This case is about the limits of governmental power. The power that the state of Georgia invoked to arrest Michael Hardwick in the bedroom of his own home is not a power to preserve public decorum. It is not a power to protect children in public or in private. It is not a power to control commerce or to outlaw the infliction of physical harm or to forbid a breach in a state-sanctioned relationship such as marriage or, indeed, to regulate the terms of a state-sanctioned relationship through laws against polygamy [having more than one marital partner at a time] or incest

67

[having sexual relations with a close relative].

The power invoked here, and I think we must be clear about it, is the power to dictate in the most intimate and, indeed, I must say, embarrassing detail how every adult, married or unmarried, in every bedroom in Georgia will behave in the closest and most intimate personal association with another adult. I think it includes all physical, sexual intimacies of a kind that are not demonstrably physically harmful, that are consensual and noncommercial in the privacy of the home.[3]

Justice Byron White then asked Tribe:

Professor, what provision of the Constitution do you rely on, or that we should rely on, to strike down this statute?

Tribe: The liberty clause of the Fourteenth Amendment, Justice White, as given further meaning and content by a course of decisions over half a century . . . if liberty means anything in our Constitution . . . it means that the power of government is limited in a way that requires an articulated rationale by government for an intrusion on freedom as personal as this. It is not a characteristic of governments devoted to liberty that they proclaim the unquestioned authority of Big Brother [state authorities such as the courts and the police] to dictate every detail of intimate life in the home.[4]

In its 5 to 4 decision, the Court decided on June 30, 1986, in favor of the state and against Hardwick. Justice White, who delivered the opinion of the Court, in which Justice O'Connor concurred, wrote, "The law is constantly based on notions of morality. Georgia's law reflects the presumed beliefs of a majority of the electorate in Georgia that homosexual sodomy is immoral and unacceptable."[5]

Justice John Paul Stevens wrote in his dissenting opinion:

> Like the statute that is challenged in this case, the rationale of the Court's opinion applies equally to the prohibited conduct regardless of whether the parties who engage in it are married or unmarried, or are of the same or different sexes. Sodomy was condemned as an odious and sinful type of behavior during the formative period of the common law. That condemnation was equally damning for heterosexual and homosexual sodomy. Moreover, it provided no special exemption for married couples. The license to cohabit and to produce legitimate offspring simply did not include any permission to engage in sexual conduct that was considered a "crime against nature . . ."

> Society has every right to encourage its individual members to follow particular traditions in expressing affection for one another and in gratifying their personal desires. It, of course, may prohibit an individual from imposing his will on another to satisfy his own selfish interests. It also may prevent an individual from interfering with, or violating, a legally sanctioned and protected relationship, such as marriage. And it may explain the relative advantages and disadvantages of different forms of intimate expression. But when individual married couples are isolated from observation by others, the way in which they voluntarily choose to conduct their intimate relations is a matter for them—not the State—to decide. The essential "liberty" that animated the development of the law . . . surely embraces the right to engage in nonreproductive, sexual conduct that others may consider offensive or immoral.

> Paradoxical [contrary] as it may seem, our prior cases thus establish that a State may not prohibit sodomy within "the sacred precincts of marital bedrooms . . ."

or, indeed, between unmarried heterosexual adults. . . .
In all events, it is perfectly clear that the State of
Georgia may not totally prohibit the conduct
proscribed by . . . the Georgia Criminal Code.

I respectfully dissent.[6]

Despite the deep convictions of the dissenting Justices,
O'Connor and a majority of the Court ruled to overturn the
Court of Appeals' decision.

Another personal liberties case over which O'Connor
presided occurred just three years later, in 1989.

The 1984 Republican National Convention held in
Dallas, Texas, attracted thousands of delegates and hundreds
of demonstrators. One small group of protestors, which called
itself the Revolutionary Communist Youth Brigade, marched
through downtown Dallas. The group was led by Gregory
Johnson. The group marched and shouted slogans over a
loudspeaker. When the group reached City Hall, Johnson
held up an American flag, which he soaked with lighter fluid
and set on fire. While the flag burned, the protesters chanted,
"Red, white, and blue, we spit on you!"[7]

The demonstration drew a large crowd. Johnson was
arrested and convicted of "desecration of a venerated object,"
which was a crime under Texas law, and sentenced to one
year in prison.

The state supreme court overruled the conviction, and the
case came before the Supreme Court in a case called *Texas* v.
Johnson. Arguing for the state was assistant district attorney
Kathi Drew.

> **Drew:** Mr. Chief Justice, and may it please the Court.
>
> The issue before this Court is whether the public
> burning of an American flag which occurred as part
> of a demonstration with political overtones is entitled

Justice O'Connor (center, with President Reagan) has had an extremely important place in history. This is not only because she was the first woman selected to be on the Supreme Court, but also because of the importance of the cases over which she has had a deciding vote.

to First Amendment protection . . .

I would like to address first the nationhood interest. We believe that preservation of the flag as a symbol of nationhood and national unity is a compelling and valid state interest. We feel very certain that Congress has the power to both adopt a national symbol and to take steps to prevent the destruction of that symbol, to protect the symbol.[8]

At this point, Justice Antonin Scalia interrupted to ask a question:

. . . Why did the defendant's actions here destroy the symbol? His actions would have been useless unless the flag was a very good symbol for what he intended to show contempt for. His action does not make it any less a symbol.

Drew: Your Honor, we believe that if a symbol over a period of time is ignored or abused that it can, in fact, lose its symbolic effect.

Scalia: I think not at all. I think when somebody does that to the flag, the flag becomes even more a symbol of the country. I mean, it seems to me you're running quite a different argument—not that he's destroying its symbolic character, but that he is showing disrespect for it, that you not just want a symbol, but you want a venerated symbol, and you don't make that argument because then you're getting into a sort of content preference. I don't see how you can argue that he's making it any less of a symbol than it was.

Drew: Your Honor, I'm forced to disagree with you. Because I believe that every desecration of the flag carried out in the manner that he did here—and certainly I don't think there can be any question that Mr. Johnson is a hard-core violator of this statue—if his actions in this case, under the facts of this case, do not constitute flag desecration, then I really am not quite certain what *would* constitute flag desecration . . . Texas is not suggesting that we can insist on respect. We are suggesting that we have the right to preserve the physical integrity of the flag so that it may serve as a symbol because its symbolic effect is diluted by certain flagrant public acts of flag desecration.[9]

At this point, O'Connor joined in the argument, forcing a concession from Drew:

I thought this statute only applied if the desecration were done in a way that the [person] knows will offend one or more other people likely to discover it.

Drew: That is correct, Your Honor.

O'Connor: There is that little added requirement [to the law], is there not?

Drew: Yes, Your Honor, that is correct.

O'Connor: Well, I thought that the Court had held that it's firmly settled under the Constitution, that the public expression of ideas may not be prohibited merely because the ideas are themselves offensive to some of their hearers.

Drew: That's correct, Your Honor.

O'Connor: And this statute seems to try to achieve exactly that.

Drew: I don't believe that it does, Your Honor, because I believe that the pivotal point is, in a way, how is the conduct effectuated, how is it done, not what an individual may be trying to say, not how onlookers perceive the action, not how the crowd reacts, but how is it done. If you take your flag into your basement in the dead of night, soak it with lighter fluid, and ignite it, you probably have not violated the

O'Connor has never been afraid to state her views. In the *Texas* v. *Johnson* case, O'Connor dissented from the majority view. She believed that the United States flag was a symbol of great worth which should be protected from harm.

statute, because the Texas statute is restricted to certain limited forms of flag desecration.[10]

At that point, Justice Scalia continued the debate with Drew in an effort to discover the state's basis for its claims.

> What is the juridical [judicial] category you're asking us to adopt in order to say we can punish this kind of speech? Just an exception for flags? It's just a—there's just a flag exception of the First Amendment?
>
> **Drew:** To a certain extent, we have made that argument in our brief. With respect to the symbolic speech standard, we believe that there are compelling state interests that will in a balancing posture override this individual's symbolic speech rights, and that preserving the flag as a symbol, because it is such a national property, is one of those.[11]

Here, O'Connor broke in with another question for the assistant district attorney.

> O'Connor: Do you suppose Patrick Henry and any of the Founding Fathers ever showed disrespect to the Union Jack [the flag of Great Britain]?
>
> **Drew:** Quite possibly, Your Honor.
>
> O'Connor: You think they had in mind then in drafting the First Amendment that it should be a prosecutable offense?
>
> **Drew:** Of course, Your Honor, one has no way of knowing whether it would be or not.[12]

After a brief concluding statement, Drew was followed by William Kunstler, the attorney arguing for Johnson. The first thing he did was to attack Drew's argument that the flag is a sacred symbol.

It's used all over for commercial purposes. I notice that Barbara Bush [the wife of former president George Bush] wore a flag scarf, for example. There are flag bikinis, there are flag everythings. There are little cocktail flags that you put into a hot dog or meatball and then throw in the garbage pail. They're flags under the Texas statute, something made out of cloth, but I think there are all sorts of flags used commercially. I'm not sure in my heart whether I think there's any control over the use of the flag, not on the criminal side anyway . . .

The Texas court of appeals [that overturned Johnson's conviction] treated this, I think, in its opinion. It said, "This statute is so broad that it may be used to punish protected conduct which has no propensity to result in breaches of the peace." Serious offense does not always result in a breach of the peace. The protest in this case did not lead to violence. And, I might add, in this protest they had policemen right along with them, undercover police officers. The crowd was not a large crowd. They estimate between one hundred, one hundred-ten, and Texas went on to say, as with most other protests of this nature, police were present at the scene . . .

I think this is a fundamental First Amendment case, that the First Amendment to the written Constitution is in jeopardy by statutes like this . . . Justice [Robert H.] Jackson said in *Barnette* [*West Virginia State Board of Education* v. *Barnette*, a case involving saluting the flag], "Those who begin coercive elimination of dissent soon find themselves eliminating dissenters. Compulsory unification of opinion achieves only the unanimity of the graveyard. The First Amendment was designed to avoid these ends by avoiding these beginnings." I think [this is] a most important case. I sense that it goes to the heart of the First Amendment, to hear things or to see things that we hate tests the First Amendment more than seeing or hearing things that we like. It wasn't designed for things we like. They never needed a First Amendment. This statute, or this amendment, was designed so that the things we hate can have a place in the marketplace of ideas and can have an area where protest can find itself. I submit that this Court should on whatever ground it feels right, should affirm the Texas court of criminal appeals with reference to this statute and this conviction. Thank you very much.[13]

On June 21, 1989, the Court struck down the Texas law by a 5 to 4 vote. Justice William Brennan, writing for the majority, said, ". . . the State emphasizes the 'special place' reserved for the flag in our Nation . . . If there is a bedrock principle underlying the First Amendment, it is that the Government may not prohibit the expression of an idea because society finds the idea . . . offensive."[14]

Justice Anthony Kennedy, concurring with Brennan, wrote, "The hard fact is that sometimes we must make decisions we do not like. We make them because they are right, right in the sense that the law and the Constitution, as we see them, compel the result."[15]

Disagreeing with the majority were Chief Justice Rehnquist and Justices White, Stevens, and O'Connor. In their dissenting opinion, they said:

> In holding this Texas statute unconstitutional, the Court ignores Justice [Oliver Wendell] Holmes' familiar aphorism that "a page of history is worth a volume of logic."

. . . For more than 200 years, the American flag has occupied a unique position as the symbol of our Nation, a uniqueness that justifies a governmental prohibition against flag burning in the way respondent Johnson did here.

At the time of the American Revolution, the flag served to unify the Thirteen Colonies at home, while obtaining recognition of national sovereignty abroad. . . .

The American flag played a central role in our Nation's most tragic conflict, when the North fought against the South. The lowering of the American flag at Fort Sumter was viewed as the start of the war. . . .

The Court [has decided] that the American flag is just another symbol, about which not only must opinions . . . be tolerated, but for which the most minimal public respect may not be [granted]. The government may conscript men into the Armed Forces where they must fight and perhaps die for the flag, but the government may not prohibit the public burning of the banner under which they fight. I would uphold the Texas statute as applied in this case.[16]

The Court's opinion helped to strengthen the scope of the First Amendment. But O'Connor and the other dissenting Justices pointed up the very special nature of the flag as a national symbol.

Following the decision, the controversy spilled out into America. Pleas for and against protection of the flag flooded Congress. O'Connor herself received thousands of letters in support of her minority view.

Finally, a few months following the decision, Congress passed the Flag Protection Act of 1989. It attempted to challenge by law the Supreme Court's ruling in *Johnson*. But in 1990, the Court found the act unconstitutional in the case *United States* v. *Eichman*. Once again, Rehnquist, White, Stevens, and O'Connor dissented.

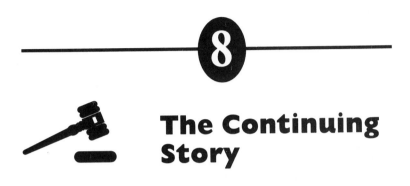

The Continuing Story

Before the beginning of the Court's 1988 term, O'Connor had gone to the doctor for a routine medical examination. The doctor found something that concerned him—a lump in one of her breasts. He sent O'Connor to a specialist who took X-rays, followed by a biopsy, the taking of a tissue sample of the lump. Within days everyone's worst fears were confirmed. Sandra Day O'Connor had breast cancer.

Two weeks after the discovery, O'Connor entered Georgetown University Hospital for surgical removal of the cancerous tissue, followed by chemotherapy, a chemical treatment to prevent the cancer's return.

Still, in typical O'Connor fashion, she had treated the episode not as a catastrophe but as a stepping-stone in life. Although some courtroom speculators and members of the press thought that O'Connor might retire from the bench, she soon made it clear that she had no intention of leaving judicial service yet.

Sandra Day O'Connor was diagnosed with breast cancer in 1988. The cancer was another obstacle that O'Connor was able to turn into a stepping-stone.

Shortly after her surgery, O'Connor issued a statement to the press. It was not flowery—merely a simple statement of the facts. As always, she got right down to the question at hand. The statement she issued told the world what O'Connor—and they—could expect in the near future.

"I underwent surgery for breast cancer," she said. "It was found to exist in a very early form and stage. The prognosis is for total recovery. I do not anticipate missing any oral arguments."[1]

She would, as usual, turn out to be correct. She had no intention of missing a case, and she did not. She carried a full workload from the day after her surgery throughout the following term, not only hearing oral arguments, but also doing all those extra duties a Supreme Court Justice is required to do. She reviewed mountains of mail, answered requests for autographed photos, made speeches, attended various social and charitable events, and administered the oath of office to various political officials, including Elizabeth Dole on becoming Secretary of Transportation and Dan Quayle on taking his position as Vice-President of the United States under President George Bush.

As O'Connor moved into her second decade on the Court, her reputation as a maverick Justice did not diminish. She voted twice to uphold the convictions of juvenile and mentally retarded offenders and twice to strike down such convictions. In each case, she wrote a separate opinion to stress that her decisions were not based upon any hard-and-fast rules but rather on each individual case.

In 1990, she voted with the majority in *Cruzan* v. *Director, Missouri Department of Health*, in which the Court overturned a Missouri Supreme Court ruling involving a permanently incapacitated patient. The Missouri court said that the patient, whose life was being sustained solely by machines, could not have those machines removed. It was a difficult case in many respects, but once again O'Connor studied the pros and cons and voted her conscience. Following the Court's decision, the machines were removed. On December 26, 1990—nearly eight years after the disabling accident that had left her unconscious—Nancy Beth Cruzan, age thirty-three, died peacefully in her bed.

That same year, O'Connor was back reviewing abortion issues—this time, in *Hodgson* v. *Minnesota*. The case involved a Minnesota law requiring that both parents be notified whenever a minor seeks an abortion. When such notification was not possible, the law required that the minor get the approval of the court.

To many, it sounded like a reasonable enough law, with just the kinds of abortion restrictions people assumed O'Connor would support. But O'Connor surprised nearly everyone by pointing out that the requirement of notifying both parents was unreasonable and thus unconstitutional in light of the large number of families in which a minor resides with only one parent or in families where the male parent has sexually abused the minor. O'Connor voted to keep the part of the law that made the consent of a judge a requirement before having an abortion. Both issues of the case were decided 5 to 4, with O'Connor voting with the majority in each one.

Another common denominator for O'Connor popped up in 1992 in the case of *Lee* v. *Weisman*. The case involved the separation of church and state.

Daniel Weisman of Providence, Rhode Island, who objected to prayers at his daughter's graduation ceremony, filed suit to have the prayers eliminated. Although the

Weismans were Jewish and the prayers were offered by a rabbi, the family felt their use in a public school graduation ceremony violated the First Amendment's separation of church and state clause.[2]

After two lower courts upheld the Weismans, the case was reviewed by the United States Supreme Court. Most observers expected the Court to overturn the lower courts' rulings and uphold the constitutionality of the prayers, since participation in them was voluntary and the prayers did not promote religion. But the Court, in a surprising 5 to 4 decision that included O'Connor, upheld the rulings.

The dissenters, including Chief Justice Rehnquist, lambasted the ruling. Justice Scalia, writing the dissent, called the decision "incoherent" and said the majority ruling would harm "an even more longstanding American tradition of nonsectarian prayer to God at public celebrations generally." He called the ruling "beyond the absurd."[3]

Writing for the majority, with O'Connor firmly behind him, Justice Kennedy expressed the Court's concern that, although the prayers were not mandatory, peer pressure might force some students to participate against their will.[4]

It was bound to be a controversial decision—once again placing O'Connor in the firestorm of public opinion. But, as she was quick to point out, it was *her* decision, and she voted the way she believed she should.

Her independent spirit has been a hallmark of O'Connor's tenure on the bench. She has at times been called a conservative, then a liberal, and even—for lack of a better term—a moderate. Yet while she seemed to bounce all over the political spectrum with her decisions, there is one issue on which O'Connor has never wavered—striking down judgements that promote sexual harassment or discrimination based upon gender.

The right of women to work without discrimination has been a lifelong rallying cry for O'Connor. She has always voted with the majority in such cases, often providing the necessary fifth vote to produce a decision.

But where other matters are concerned—everything from antitrust cases to cases involving First Amendment freedoms, civil rights, and abortion—she has been decidedly unpredictable. O'Connor's approach to voting is singular; she does not take her decisions lightly. On the contrary, it's that she wants to balance carefully her opinions on a case-by-case basis.

Thus O'Connor's tendency to make independent and politically moderate judgments gives her an increasing amount of influence on a Court that grows more polarized—with half the Justices liberal and the other half conservative—each day. This is precisely the role she has always wished to play.

Recently, O'Connor has become active in yet another role—that of judicial reformer. Working closely with the American Bar Association and Attorney General Janet Reno, she outlined a plan for changing America's civil justice system.

Inspired to support changes in the nation's judicial system due to dwindling resources, delays in bringing cases to trial, and a general lack of faith in the system by the American public, O'Connor addressed the Summit on Civil Justice Improvements held in Washington, D.C., in December 1993. She told the attorneys in attendance that the legal profession "has served our country well in the past, and we can continue to serve it well today. But we cannot serve it by going on with business as usual."[5]

O'Connor believed in judging each case independently rather than upon previously set rules or guidelines. Here, she is signing a document while President Reagan watches.

O'Connor, especially concerned about the growing lack of civility among lawyers, went on to warn the summit, "The justice system cannot function effectively when those charged with its function cannot be polite to one another. If there is one thing on which we should agree, it is the need to put civility back in our profession."[6]

In considering the need to implement changes, the ABA Committee on Civil Justice Improvements broke down the proposed changes into four main categories. These include the following:

While the ABA considers changes to the judicial system, Sandra Day O'Connor continues with her work on the

1) The need for establishing pretrial settlement procedures and facilities. Such procedures and facilities would allow litigants to settle an issue before the case comes to court, thus reducing the caseload and lightening the strain on America's courts.

2) The adoption of a more effective summary judgment rule. This rule would allow the court to issue a verdict in certain cases without having to send the issue to a jury for decision. This rule could likewise simplify courtroom procedures and reduce caseloads.

3) The establishment of pre-complaint notices. This would require plaintiffs to give prior notice to prospective defendants of pending suits, once again allowing for the possibility of a greater number of settlements outside of court.

4) The offering of settlement procedure incentives. This process would entice litigants to accept various alternative measures of resolving a dispute without going to court.

bench. She often spends ten to twelve grueling hours a day hearing arguments, researching legal precedents, considering the merits of various cases, and weighing all the factors of a case in light of her moral, legal, and political principles. It's a tough way to earn a living, but it's the best—in fact, the *only*—way for the Supreme Court to function.

So long as O'Connor continues to vote her conscience and not someone's preconceived notion or political ideology, she is doing what America intended. The Supreme Court was established in the Constitution, through the passage of the Judiciary Act of 1789.

Ironically, as she has gained insight into the workings of the Court, she has adopted one of the prime philosophies of her chief mentor and advocate, Thurgood Marshall. Speaking on the ever-changing issues and interpretation of the Constitution required by a Supreme Court Justice, she said, "There is never an absolute end to any issue . . . there is a continuing dialogue between the Court, the Congress, and the nation as a whole."[7]

Chronology

1930—Sandra Day is born in El Paso, Texas.

1946—Sandra Day graduates from high school in El Paso.

1950—Sandra Day graduates *magna cum laude* from Stanford University.

1952—Sandra Day graduates third in her class from Stanford Law School; becomes deputy county attorney in San Mateo, California; marries John Jay O'Connor, III.

1954—Sandra Day O'Connor begins two-year service as civilian lawyer for U.S. Army in Frankfurt, W. Germany.

1957—O'Connor gives birth to first of three sons; opens law practice in Maryvale, Arizona.

1960—O'Connor gives birth to the second of her sons.

1962—O'Connor gives birth to the third and last of her sons.

1965—O'Connor becomes an Arizona assistant attorney general.

1969—O'Connor is appointed to Arizona State Senate.

1970—O'Connor is elected to first of two full terms in Arizona State Senate.

1973—O'Connor becomes Arizona State Senate majority leader.

1974—O'Connor is elected judge of Arizona Superior Court.

1979—O'Connor is appointed to Arizona Court of Appeals.

1981—O'Connor is nominated by President Ronald Reagan to United States Supreme Court; confirmed by United

States Senate in September; takes seat as America's first femal associate Justice; writes first opinion, *Watt* v. *Energy Action.*

1986—O'Connor votes with the majority in the landmark decision, *Bowers* v. *Hardwick.*

1988—O'Connor learns she has breast cancer; undergoes successful treatment.

1989—O'Connor votes with the minority in landmark decision, *Texas* v. *Johnson.*

2000—O'Connor continues to vote with her conscience.

Chapter Notes

Chapter 1
1. Peter W. Huber, *Sandra Day O'Connor* (New York: Chelsea House Publishers, 1990), p. 14.
2. Ibid., pp. 14–15.
3. Ibid.
4. Swearing in of Sandra Day O'Connor, Supreme Court of the United States, September 25, 1981.

Chapter 2
1. Judith Bentley, *Justice Sandra Day O'Connor* (New York: Julian Messner, 1983), p. 6.
2. Ibid., p. 7.
3. Ibid., p. 2.
4. Ibid., p. 9.

Chapter 3
1. Beverly Gehrman, *Sandra Day O'Connor: Justice for All* (New York: Viking, 1991), p. 14.
2. Ibid.
3. Judith Bentley, *Justice Sandra Day O'Connor* (New York: Julian Messner, 1983), pp. 16–17.
4. Ibid., p. 17.
5. Ibid., p. 18.

Chapter 4
1. Judith Bentley, *Justice Sandra Day O'Connor* (New York: Julian Messner, 1983), p. 28.
2. Peter W. Huber, *Sandra Day O'Connor* (New York: Chelsea House Publishers, 1990) p. 33.
3. Beverly Gehrman, *Sandra Day O'Connor: Justice for All* (New York: Viking, 1991), p. 31.

4. Huber, p. 37.

5. Gehrman, pp. 31–32.

6. Judith Bentley, *Justice Sandra Day O'Connor* (New York: Julian Messner, 1983), p. 52.

7. Huber, p. 40.

8. Ibid., p. 41.

9. Eric Foner and John A. Garraty, eds., *The Reader's Companion to American History* (Boston: Houghton Mifflin Co., 1991), p. 356.

10. Huber, p. 42.

11. Bentley, p. 57.

Chapter 5

1. Peter W. Huber, *Sandra Day O'Connor* (New York: Chelsea House Publishers, 1990), p. 46.

2. Beverly Gehrman, *Sandra Day O'Connor: Justice for All* (New York: Viking, 1991), p. 41.

3. Ibid., p. 46.

Chapter 6

1. Judith Bentley, *Justice Sandra Day O'Connor* (New York: Julian Messner, 1983), p. 86.

2. Ibid., p. 89.

3. Peter W. Huber, *Sandra Day O'Connor* (New York: Chelsea House Publishers, 1990), p. 57.

4. Ibid., p. 59.

5. Bentley, p. 86.

6. Ibid., p. 94.

7. Huber, p. 103.

8. Steven H. Gifis, *Law Dictionary*, 3rd edition (Hauppauge, N.Y.: Barron's, 1991), p. 339.

9. Ibid.

10. *Lynch* v. *Donnelly*, Majority Opinion, Chief Justice Warren Burger, U.S. Supreme Court, 1984.

11. *Lynch* v. *Donnelly*, Minority Opinion, U.S. Supreme Court, 1984.

12. *Lynch* v. *Donnelly*, Majority Opinion, Justice Sandra Day O'Connor, U.S. Supreme Court, 1984.

13. *Thornton* v. *Caldor*, Majority Opinion, U.S. Supreme Court, 1985.

14. *Akron* v. *Akron Center for Reproductive Health*, Minority Opinion of Justice Sandra Day O'Connor, Justices White and Rehnquist joining, U.S. Supreme Court, 1983.

15. James W. Ely, Jr., Joel B. Grossman, and William M. Wiecek, eds., *The Oxford Companion to The Supreme Court of the United States* (New York: Oxford University Press, 1992), p. 921.

16. Ibid., p. 922.

17. *Webster* v. *Reproductive Health Services*, Majority Opinion, Justice Sandra Day O'Connor, 1989.

18. "A Tribute to Justice Thurgood Marshall," *Stanford Law Review*, Special Issue, June 1992, pp. 1219–1220.

19. *City of Richmond* v. *J.A. Croson Company*, Majority Opinion, Justice Sandra Day O'Connor, U.S. Supreme Court, 1989.

20. Ibid.

21. *City of Richmond* v. *J.A. Croson Company*, Minority Opinion, Justice Thurgood Marshall, U.S. Supreme Court, 1989.

22. *City of Richmond* v. *J.A. Croson Company*, Majority Opinion, Justice Sandra Day O'Connor, U.S. Supreme Court, 1989.

23. Carl T. Rowan, *Dream Makers, Dream Breakers: The World of Justice Thurgood Marshall* (Boston: Little, Brown and Company, 1993), p. 440.

24. Ibid., p. 439.

Chapter 7

1. *Bowers* v. *Hardwick*, Oral Arguments, U.S. Supreme Court, 1986.

2. Ibid.

3. Ibid.

4. Ibid.

5. *Bowers* v. *Hardwick*, Majority Opinion, U.S. Supreme Court, 1986.

6. Maureen Harrison and Steve Gilbert, eds., *Landmark*

Decisions of the United States Supreme Court II (Beverly Hills, Calif.: Excellent Books, 1992), pp. 139–144.

7. Irons and Guitton, *May It Please the Court* (New York: New Press, 1993), p. 152.

8. *Texas* v. *Johnson*, Oral Arguments, U.S. Supreme Court, 1989.

9. Ibid.

10. Ibid.

11. Ibid.

12. Ibid.

13. Ibid.

14. *Texas* v. *Johnson*, Majority Opinion of Justice William Brennan, U.S. Supreme Court, 1989.

15. *Texas* v. *Johnson*, Majority Opinion of Justice Anthony Kennedy, U.S. Supreme Court, 1989.

16. *Texas* v. *Johnson*, Minority Opinion of Justice William Rehnquist, Justices White and O'Connor joining, U.S. Supreme Court, 1989.

Chapter 8

1. Peter W. Huber, *Sandra Day O'Connor* (New York: Chelsea House Publishers, 1990), p. 95.

2. "Court Decision on Prayer," *ABA Journal*, July 1992, p. 141.

3. *Lee* v. *Weisman*, Minority Opinion of Justice Antonin Scalia, Justices Rehnquist, White, and Thomas joining, U.S. Supreme Court, 1992.

4. *Lee* v. *Weisman*, Majority Opinion of Justice Anthony Kennedy, Justices O'Connor, Blackmun, Stevens, and Souter joining, U.S. Supreme Court, 1992.

5. James Podgers, "Changes Sought in Civil Justice System," *ABA Journal*, February 1994, p. 112.

6. Ibid.

7. Beverly Gehrman, *Sandra Day O'Connor: Justice for All* (New York: Viking, 1991), p. 52.

Glossary

amicus curiae—Friend of the Court, or one who gives information to the Court pertaining to some matter of law that is in doubt.

argument—A course of reasoning intended to persuade others to believe the same way.

attorney general—The chief law officer of the federal government and of each state's government.

brief—A written argument used by a lawyer to present the basic facts of the client's case, including a statement of the legal questions involved, the law that the lawyer would like to have applied, and what decision he or she wants from the court.

civil rights—Equal rights given to all people by laws enacted by civilized communities.

concurring opinion—An opinion that basically agrees with the majority opinion, but that is written to express a different view of the issues, to explain a particular judge's opinion, or to detail a point that a judge wants to point out more specifically than the majority opinion does.

court of appeals—A court of review having jurisdiction to reevaluate a law as it applies to a particular case.

decision—A final determination arrived at after consideration or a course of action decided upon.

defendant—A person who defends himself or herself against a suit.

determination—A decision by a court.

dissenting opinion—An opinion that disagrees with the majority decision made of a case by the court.

hearing—A proceeding where evidence is taken in order to determine facts of a case and reach a decision on the basis of that evidence.

indictment—A written accusation, drawn up and submitted to a grand jury by the prosecuting attorney, charging one or more persons with a crime.

integration—The mixing of different races.

judgment—The final determination of the rights of the parties to a lawsuit.

majority opinion—An opinion that is joined by a majority of the court.

opinion—The reason given for a court's judgment, finding, or conclusion.

petition—A formal written request for something to be done.

petitioner—One who presents a petition to a court.

plaintiff—The person who initially brings a suit.

segregation—The separation of different races.

separate-but-equal doctrine—The belief that separate facilities for whites and blacks are acceptable so long as the facilities are mostly equal.

solicitor general—A person appointed by the president to assist the attorney general in performing legal duties.

writ of mandamus—A court order demanding that something be done.

Further Reading

Bentley, Judith. *Justice Sandra Day O'Connor*. New York: Julian Messner, 1983.

Berger, Raoul. *Congress* vs. *The Supreme Court*. New York: Bantam Books, 1973.

Friendly, Fred. W., and Martha J. H. Elliott. *The Constitution— That Delicate Balance*. New York: Random House, 1984.

Greene, Carol. *Sandra Day O'Connor: First Woman on the Supreme Court*. Chicago: Childrens Press, 1982.

Lawson, Don. *Landmark Supreme Court Cases*. Hillside, NJ: Enslow, 1987.

Tribe, Laurence H. *God Save This Honorable Court: How the Choice of Supreme Court Justices Can Change Our Lives*. New York: Random House, 1985.

Woods, Harold, and Geraldine Woods. *Equal Justice: A Biography of Sandra Day O'Connor*. Minneapolis: Dillon Press, 1987.

Woodward, Bob, and Scott Armstrong. *The Brethren*. New York: Simon & Schuster, 1979.

Index

About the Author

D.J. Herda is a widely published author of over sixty books for young people. In addition to his career as a writer, Mr. Herda is an accomplished photographer, painter and sculptor whose works currently appear in galleries and shows throughout North America.